Looking Good

ACCESSORIES

by Arlene C. Rourke

Rourke Publications, Inc.
Vero Beach, FL 32964

WHAT ARE ACCESSORIES?

Accessories can make or break an outfit. They are as important as clothing in defining your look. Accessories pull an outfit together. They give it polish and pizzazz. The wise choice of accessories can give an otherwise boring outfit uniqueness and originality. On the other hand, poorly chosen accessories can make even the most expensive, high quality clothing look tacky or inappropriate.

What are accessories? Briefly defined, accessories are any items you wear or carry which are not major articles of clothing. Accessories include:

shoes
hosiery
handbags
gloves
hats
belts
scarves
jewelry
fragrance
eyeglasses

Accessories hold your look together by the skillful use of color, texture, and pattern in strategic places.

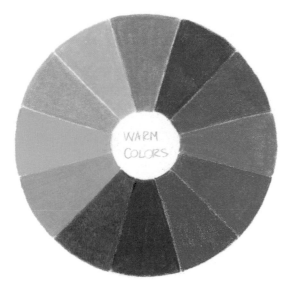

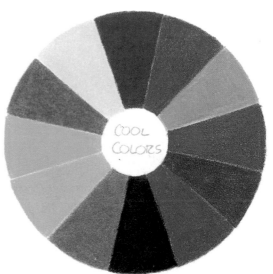

Color: Reds, oranges, and yellows are called *warm colors*. They draw the eye to themselves. Greens and blues are called *cool colors*. They do not call attention to themselves. Dark colors make things look smaller. Light or bright colors make things look bigger.

6

Does this scene sound familiar? You're dressing for school or a date. You've got your clothes on and your hair done. You take one last look in the mirror to see if all is right. No, it isn't quite right. Your look "needs something." Do you just throw on a scarf as you rush out the door, hoping for the best? Or, do you look in a mirror (preferably full length) and ask yourself, "What does this outfit really need to bring it to life?"

Do yourself a favor and take the time to put on the last touches. The right belt might be just what you need to finish off the waist. Colorful, textured hose or bright, geometric earrings can add just the right punch to an otherwise simple outfit. A gold or silver bracelet could add just the right bit of shine.

What to Look for When Buying Accessories

Remember, your accessories should enhance *you*. Find out what your style is and work with it. Some girls love lots of jewelry and it looks right on them. Some girls prefer simple pearl earrings and a bracelet; they feel overdressed with anything more. Go with what makes you comfortable. You should wear your clothes; they should not wear you.

Color in accessories is just as important as color in your basic outfit. Accessory colors should complement your skin color and your outfit. That doesn't mean that you have to wear only one color at a time. That would be boring. Check the chart on page 6 for color families and complementary colors.

Texture is the *weight* and *weave* (or *knit*) of the fabric. Texture can range from delicate silks to rough tweeds.

8

Texture is the *weave* or *knit* of a garment or accessory. To a large degree, the texture of a garment determines its mood. For example, silky or lacy outfits are usually reserved for special occasions. Fine quality woolens in flannels, plaids, and tweeds have a more classic or businesslike feeling. Denim jeans, T-shirts, and sweats indicate a sporty or relaxed, laid-back mood.

Quality of material is important if you are spending a lot of money for an item which you plan to wear for a long time. Good quality accessories, like anything else, can be very expensive. Try to buy the best quality accessories you can. A leather handbag or leather shoes in a neutral color will last a long time and always look good. Tacky fad accessories will soon be thrown away.

Scale and proportion have to do with the size relationship between your accessories and your basic outfit. A tiny gold chain would get lost on a big, bulky sweater. Choose a fairly large necklace or a large pin instead. Oversized beads are inappropriate with a silk blouse. It would be better to wear a delicate pendant or a small string of pearls.

Uniqueness of design means that the accessory is rare and unusual. Maybe you're the type of girl who likes to wear the latest fad item that *everyone else* is wearing. In that case, uniqueness might not be an important consideration for you. However, some people pride themselves on wearing something which no one else has.

GEOMETRIC

NON-GEOMETRIC

POLKA DOTS

PAISLEY

STRIPES

FLORAL

PLAIDS

BATIK — ANIMAL

Pattern is the *design* of the fabric. The size and type of pattern you wear depends mostly on your body build.

10

Pattern is the *design* of an accessory. Checks, plaids, stripes, paisleys, and florals are all examples of patterns. When choosing patterns in accessories, keep in mind the same common sense ideas you would use in choosing clothing. For example, large girls should stay away from "cute," itsy-bitsy patterns which would get lost on them. On the other hand, small girls should avoid huge prints which would dwarf them.

> **TIP:** Keep your accessories in the same family with regard to color, style, and mood. Colors should not clash. An outfit cannot be dressy and sporty at the same time.

Appropriateness has to do with an accessory's suitability. Does the accessory suit the season, the outfit, and the occasion? Fancy gold jewelry is too dressy with a summer shorts outfit. Black net pantyhose at a basketball game is simply inappropriate. However, simple silver jewelry with a jeans outfit can be very effective.

> **TIP:** Instead of spending a fortune on each new fad in clothing, choose simple, classic clothes. Update them with the latest accessories.

Let's explore the major categories of accessories and see what's right for you.

Shoes

There is an incredible variety of shoes available to you. Shoes come in every color, fabric, and design for every sport or occasion. Walking into a shoe store is like walking through Wonderland. Some people become shoe fanatics and buy shoes that they can't use and will never wear. That can be an expensive mistake. How do you decide what's right and what's enough?

Think about what you use shoes for. Of course, you'll need school shoes. If you're an athlete, you'll need sport shoes. You'll need dressy shoes for special occasions, and a few pairs of shoes for everyday wear.

> **TIP:** If your feet are still growing, don't get bogged down with a whole wardrobe of shoes that will be too small in no time. Buy shoes as you need them.

Buying shoes Buy shoes carefully. You usually can't return them, unless they haven't been worn. Neutral colors are a wise choice because they go with just about everything. Neutral colors include tan, black, gray, bone, white, and navy. Sometimes red is considered a neutral color.

Leather is long lasting. Suede is beautiful, but it gets dirty easily. It is hard to clean, and it can wear off in spots. Fabric shoes also soil easily and generally do not last long.

If you have any doubts about your shoe size, ask the salesperson to measure *both* feet. It is not unusual for a person to have one foot slightly larger than the other. Walk around the store to see if the shoes feel right. Don't believe any salesperson who says that a tight pair of shoes will stretch. They won't. What they will do is drive you crazy until you finally throw them away!

Here are a few points which will help you select the right shoes:

    If you're wondering what heel height is appropriate with an outfit, here's a rule of thumb: The shorter the skirt, the lower the heel; the longer the skirt, the higher the heel.

    If you have permission to wear heels, don't abuse the privilege. Heels that are too high for you will throw you off balance and give you a pained expression.

    Keep shoes in good repair. Have worn-down shoes repaired. Clean and polish when necessary.

    Shoes with a V-shaped front add length to your legs.

The **flat** is a simple, low heeled shoe. Flats can be sporty or dressy, depending on the material and decoration. Flats should not be perfectly flat. For good posture, the heel should be about ¾″ high.

The **pump** is the classic high-heeled shoe. Pumps come in all heel heights and materials. They may be perfectly plain or dressed up with bows, buckles, rhinestones, and so on. Depending on their style, they are appropriate for many occasions.

The **T-strap** can be formal or informal. The area below the ankle is covered with two strips of material in a definite "T" design. *Warning:* T-straps tend to make your feet and ankles look broader. Stay away from them if you have heavy legs.

Sling-back shoes are another variation on the pump. The sling-back lacks a solid back. Instead it has a strip of material below the ankle, like a sandal. *Warning:* Because the heel tends to wobble, sling-backs are only for the sure-footed.

Sandals are shoes made of straps. Sandals can have either a high or a low heel. They are great in the summertime since they allow the feet to breathe. High-heeled sandals give a more sophisticated look. Plastic sandals come in a variety of colors and are inexpensive. Since there's no worry of water ruining them, they are great for the beach.

Sneakers are available in many colors and designs. If you are an athlete or participate regularly in a sport, buy a shoe that is designed for that sport. Not only will you look like you know what you are doing, but you need the support and protection the appropriate shoe gives you.

Boots are used by many people for a variety of purposes. They range from hard working cowboy boots to high fashion high-heeled boots. Boots go especially well with jeans or a peasant shirt.

Demi boots are half boots. The word *demi* means "half." Because they do not cover the lower leg, they tend to be used more as "fun" boots rather than for warmth or practicality.

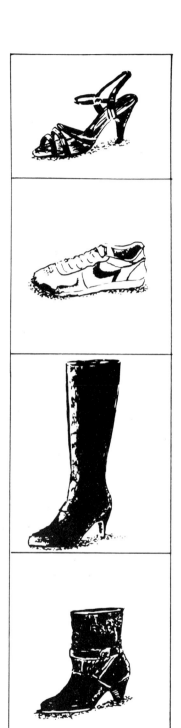

15

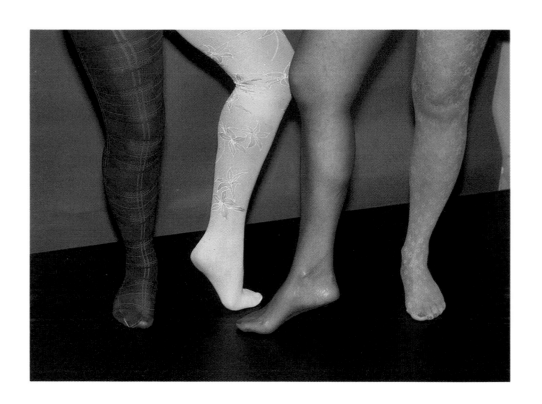

Hosiery

It is a pity that some people wear the same old boring socks or stockings with every outfit. Hosiery comes in so many colors and patterns that it can be a truly exciting contribution to your wardrobe.

Hosiery should always be chosen with the total look of the outfit in mind. A sporty wool pantsuit can be perked up with a snappy pair of argyle socks. A lacy pair of pantyhose can make a plain party dress so much more special. On the other hand, if an outfit has a lot of patterns or colors, choose a pair of simple hose. Try to match one of the colors in the outfit. When in doubt about color, choose a neutral color.

Rules of thumb regarding hosiery:

dark stockings have a slimming effect
diamond and horizontal shapes make the leg look wider
the higher the heel, the sheerer the hose
stockings and shoes in the same color or tint make the legs
 look longer
leg warmers add weight and make the legs look fatter

Handbags

Do you really need all those things you lug around in your handbag? Dump the whole mess out on a table and take a good, hard look at it. Eliminate the useless items. Group together all the things which are used for the same purpose. Get a pouch for your cosmetics. Use an organizer for your school supplies. You may find that you can really lighten your load.

When choosing a handbag, remember what we said about scale and proportion. Not only should your handbag be in scale with your outfit, it should be in scale with *you*. A tall girl in a bulky sweater carrying a big coach bag is in proportion. A short girl in the same outfit looks overwhelmed. Before buying a handbag, always check yourself in a full length mirror. Don't buy anything that is out of proportion.

The days when the handbag had to *exactly* match the shoes are over. However, in order to look well dressed, your bag and shoes should somehow look as though they *belong* together. Maybe they are made of the same material, or the same color, or the same pattern. Try to find something that ties them — and your whole look — together.

Gloves

Most people go for neutral colors in gloves. This is because gloves last a long time and have to go with everything. Good leather gloves are your best bet in winter. Cashmere is also wonderfully warm and usually cheaper than leather.

Choose gloves with pointed fingers since they give the illusion of long, graceful hands. Mittens should not be worn by anyone over the age of ten!

TIP: Most fad clothes go out of style very quickly. Accessories such as gloves, hosiery, and hats are usually not expensive and can give you an up-to-the-minute look without costing a fortune. So, don't be afraid to experiment.

20

Hats

Hats are making a comeback after being out of fashion for quite a while. Luckily, hats come in just about every style and mood so just about anyone can find the right hat.

Hats that are bought for fashion (as opposed to hats that are bought for warmth or protection) should be chosen on the basis of face shape and body build. Remember scale and proportion?

If you are short, steer toward hats with crowns. They give the illusion of height. Stay away from the wide-brimmed, "picture" hats that emphasize your height. Berets and caps are more your size.

For special occasions, a big, dramatic hat can give a tall girl a sense of presence and drama. Imagine a girl in a beautiful picture hat and a chiffon dress at a summer wedding reception.

Always consider the shape of your face when choosing a hat. Don't buy a hat in the same shape as your face. On the opposite page you will see some face shapes and the appropriate hats for them.

TIP: Don't be afraid to look for hats — or other accessories — in unusual places. The boys' department of a good department store can provide a unique assortment of hats in a variety of styles and colors.

Belts

Belts add texture, color, and polish to an outfit. If chosen wisely, they can also minimize figure flaws, four of which are shown below:

short waisted: Match your belt to your shirt color. It gives the illusion of greater space between the shoulder and the waist. Avoid wide, fancy belts.

long waisted: Choose a wider belt in the same color as your skirt or pants. This creates an illusion of greater space in the lower part of your body.

big hips: Never buckle your belt too tightly. A tiny, pushed-in waist will only make your hips look bigger.

too short: Wear belts in the same color as your outfit. *Never* wear a contrasting color at the waist. It cuts you in half. Choose belts that form a vertical line. For example, sashes which hang below the belt line.

TIP: If you're wearing a belt which has a large, fancy buckle, let that be your only ornament. Lots of jewelry added to that would be too much.

Scarves

Scarves add punch and excitement to an outfit. They come in so many shapes and sizes that they can be used in a variety of ways — as bows, belts, ascots, bandanas, mufflers, sarongs, kerchiefs, and pocket handkerchiefs.

Keep the pattern and texture of the scarf in relation to its purpose. Silk and lace scarves are generally worn with dressy clothes. Nubby or knitted scarves are for informal wear.

TIP: If you have a short neck, tie your scarf low around your neck. It gives the illusion of a longer neck.

Tie the colors of your outfit together with the color of the scarf. If there are many colors in your outfit, you might choose a solid color scarf in one of your outfit colors. A one-color outfit would benefit from a scarf in a contrasting or complementary color.

Be careful of color if you wear a scarf around your neck. Its color will reflect on your face. Muddy or uncomplementary colors can be very unflattering. Pink, peach, coral, white, and off-white work best for most people.

TIP: If you want to hide a big bust, wear a dark colored blouse and a colorful scarf at the neck. The scarf will attract the eye's attention.

Jewelry

Jewelry is probably the first thing people think about when the word *accessory* is mentioned. Jewelry, of course, is an eye-catcher. Don't ever put a piece of jewelry on a part of the body you're trying to hide.

Most people own a watch. Watches are both practical and ornamental. Buy the best watch you can afford. You'll be wearing it for a long time. Select a watchband that goes with the clothes in your wardrobe.

Jewelry can be dramatic or subtle, charming or outrageous. It is an extension of your personality. Choose your jewelry well because it says a lot about you. Chunky, geometric jewelry makes a definite fashion statement. It is particularly effective on tall girls. Don't go overboard with it. Big earrings, necklace, and bracelets all at once are overkill.

Some girls like the soft, romantic look of antique jewelry, pearls, and cameos. They are beautiful on silks, satins, velvets, and on lacy Victorian dresses. Try looking for antique jewelry in thrift stores.

Pearls are classics, and they look good on everyone. When in doubt, wear pearls. Treat natural or cultured pearls tenderly because they scratch easily. Wrap them carefully when you're not using them. Always put your pearl jewelry on *after* you use hair spray or cologne. Harsh chemicals can eat into the surface of your pearls, causing them to become dull. If any spray should get on your pearls, rinse it off as soon as possible with clear, warm water. Dry the pearls gently with a clean towel.

Inexpensive costume jewelry is useful to experiment with until you decide what your likes and dislikes are. Try to develop an appreciation for fine jewelry — gold, silver, pearls, precious, or semi-precious gems. It may be a long time before you can afford such things. However, a few pieces of genuine jewelry will always look good, and they will last a lifetime.

Fragrance

Fragrance gives you the finishing touch. It creates an aura about you. Even when you are no longer in a room, your fragrance lingers. Because it becomes something like your own trademark, the greatest care should be taken in choosing a fragrance. Each person has her own body chemistry, which blends with the fragrance she wears. That is why the same fragrance will smell different on different persons.

Fragrance comes in three strengths: *perfume,* which is the strongest and most expensive; *eau de toilette;* and *cologne,* which is the weakest. There are many types of fragrances. The basic types are *florals, greens* (woodsy), *musks* (heavy), and *orientals* (exotic, spicy, sweet). Girls and young women tend to prefer the floral and greens types of fragrances. Leave the musky and oriental scents to older women.

Apply fragrance to your pulse spots — inside the wrists, behind the knees, around the temples. Too much fragrance is worse than none at all. When in doubt, use less.

Eyeglasses

Stop complaining about having to wear eyeglasses! With the beautiful eyewear available today, glasses can be a great fashion asset. It takes time and patience to choose the right frame for you. Select frames in a shape other than your face shape. Your eyebrows should be covered by the frame. If you have a large nose, try a frame with a low bridge. For a broad nose, try a frame with a dark-toned bridge.

BIBLIOGRAPHY

Fashion Smarts, Kirsten Brown and Susan Cooney Evans. Playboy Press Paperbacks, New York.

Real Clothes, J.C. Saures and Susan Osborn. William Morrow and Company, Inc. New York.

Dress Better for Less, Vicki Audette. Meadowbrook Press, Deephaven, Minnesota.

Glamour's Success Book, Barbara Coffey. Simon and Schuster, New York.

Dressing Rich, Leah Feldon. G.P. Putnam's Sons, New York.

"The Right Brights," Woman's Day. July 23, 1985.

"Accessories Fashion Design," Vogue Magazine. July 1983, p. 148.

Short Chic, Allison Kyle Leopold and Anne Marie Cloutier. Rawson, Wade Publishers, Inc. New York.

"Shades of Summer," Seventeen. June 1986, p. 138.

"If the Shoe Fits, Pair It," Seventeen. November 1985, p. 122.

"Buckle Up," Seventeen. October 1985, p. 34.

"Vision Quest," Seventeen. October 1985, p. 137.

"Gloves by the Handful," Seventeen. January 1986, p. 18.

INDEX